CONTENTS

CHAPTER ONE 5

A RIVER CITY

CHAPTER TWO 11

EGYPTIAN KINGDOMS

CHAPTER THREE 17

EGYPTIAN CULTURE

CHAPTER FOUR 23

THE FALL OF EGYPT

HISTORY HAPPENED HERE 28

EVENTS DURING ANCIENT EGYPT 29

GLOSSARY 30

FIND OUT MORE 31

INDEX 32

The Nile River has always been an important part of life in Egypt—from ancient times to today.

CHAPTER ONE

A RIVER CITY

Like many ancient civilizations, ancient Egypt **developed** near a river. This river, called the Nile, was important for many reasons. It gave people fresh water, and the Egyptians could use boats to move people and things from place to place. Also, each year from July through September, the Nile River flooded the nearby land. These floods were dangerous, or unsafe, but they also helped turn desert into farmland along the riverbanks. Early Egyptians used the rich soil along the Nile's riverbanks to grow grain and raise pigs, sheep, and cattle.

A LONG HISTORY

Egypt is in the northeastern part of Africa, and **experts** know that the first humans migrated out of Africa about 100,000 years ago. It makes sense that some of them lived in Egypt. Experts also know that people started making villages in Egypt about 7,000 years ago. These grew into a civilization.

Over time, the Egyptian civilization grew into two kingdoms. Lower Egypt was located in the **river delta** of the north. Upper Egypt was located in the drier valley to the south. The names "Upper" and "Lower" come from the direction in which the Nile flows. The kings of Upper Egypt wore a white crown. The

This carving from an Egyptian temple shows the person in the middle being given the double crown of Egypt. On the left, the person is wearing the white crown of Upper Egypt. On the right, the person is wearing the red crown of Lower Egypt.

kings of Lower Egypt wore a red crown. When the two lands later **united**, a double crown was created that was both red and white.

MAKING GUESSES

Archaeologists have had to make a lot of guesses about the history of ancient Egypt. They know that the kingdoms were united around 3100 BCE during a time called the Early Dynastic Period. A dynasty is a period of time when a single family rules. However, experts disagree about how Egypt was united. A Greek historian named Manetho wrote a history of Egypt around 323 BCE, but some modern historians think some of it is wrong or incomplete.

Ancient Greek and Roman people wrote that Memphis,

This carving is called the Narmer **Palette**. It shows Narmer wearing the white crown of Upper Egypt.

WRITTEN RECORDS

The earliest written records in human history date back to about 5,000 years ago. Ancient Egypt and ancient Sumer developed writing systems at almost the same time, but they were nothing alike. The ancient Sumerians created a wedge-shaped system called cuneiform, and the Egyptians created hieroglyphs, or picture writing. Only the most educated people could read or write this script. Over time, the Egyptians created three other forms of writing that common people could use.

the capital of Egypt, was founded in Lower Egypt around 2925 BCE by a mythical king called Menes. People who study Egypt's history think Menes was a real king called Narmer. However, in the 2010s, modern archaeologists found writing carved in stone in Egypt's Sinai Desert. These carvings were made by ancient Egyptians who were sent out by the early rulers to find good places to mine for copper. The carvings prove that Memphis existed long before Narmer was even born. The ruler at the time the carvings were made was called Iry-Hor, but experts think the White Walls, another name for Memphis, might have been a city even before he came to power.

This map shows some of the most important places in ancient Egypt.

A COMMON MYTH

Many people believe the pyramids were built by enslaved people. However, archaeologists have found proof that this is not true. **Sites** uncovered near the pyramids show that the pyramid builders lived together close to where they were working. Written records show that they were fed well, paid for their work, and given health care. The workers took turns living at the work site and went home when it was not their turn to work.

THE MIDDLE KINGDOM

Around 2125 BCE, the ruler of Thebes, the city in Upper Egypt, finally beat the ruler of the Lower Egyptian city. This ruler, whose name was Mentuhotep II, reunited Egypt and ruled both parts of it. Thebes became the most important city in Egypt. A later ruler named Amenemhat I created Egypt's first army. Because life was peaceful again, people could focus on creating art and writing.

Over time, the government grew weaker, and a group of people called the Hyksos grew stronger. The Hyksos lived in Lower Egypt, but they were not Egyptian. Experts are not sure exactly where they came from, but their best guess is that they came from an area around the countries that are now Syria and Palestine. The Hyksos grew so much stronger than the Egyptian government that they took over most of Lower Egypt. Around the same time this was happening, the kingdom of Kush rose to power in Nubia, an area south of Egypt. Kush took over part of Lower Egypt, and the Middle Kingdom period ended around 1650 BCE.

Pharaohs often wore fake beards as a **symbol** of their connection to the gods. Even though Queen Hatshepsut was a woman, she wanted a beard added to statues of her, such as this one.

THE NEW KINGDOM

During the Second Intermediate Period, the Egyptians tried to take back their land from the Hyksos and the Nubians. They finally did this around 1550 BCE. Prince Ahmose I of Thebes took back control and reunited Egypt again. The New Kingdom period, like the two kingdoms before it, was stable and peaceful. King Thutmose I expanded Egypt's borders, and Hatshepsut—a female pharaoh—expanded trade with other civilizations. Egypt's best trading partner was a kingdom called Punt. Some experts today think this was probably the modern-day country of Somalia and may have included parts of what are now Ethiopia and Djibouti. However, the Egyptians never wrote down where it was, so we can't know for sure! Historians made their guess because the descriptions of Punt's main city almost exactly match the descriptions of an ancient city with a similar name in Somalia.

These times of peace allowed Egyptians to develop a unique, or special, way of life. They had their own religion, or belief system. They developed their own styles of art. They also had their own calendar, and science was very important to them. We know all of this from what the Egyptians who lived during these times left behind.

This temple carving shows a pharaoh giving gifts to the sun god, Ra.

CHAPTER THREE
EGYPTIAN CULTURE

Religion was an important part of ancient Egyptian **culture**. Egyptian religion was polytheistic, which means the people believed in more than one god. Egyptians thought these gods created and controlled their world. Pharaohs were also worshipped because they were seen as a connection between the gods and humans.

THE ANCIENT EGYPTIAN RELIGION

Religion played a huge part in the everyday life of the ancient Egyptians. They built large temples for their gods and for the pharaohs, and priests and priestesses were important people. The Egyptians believed priests could do magic to either heal people or put curses on their enemies. This magic came from a god called Heka, which was also the ancient Egyptian word for magic.

Other important gods and goddesses were Amun, the king of the gods; Osiris, the god of the afterlife; Ra, a sun god with the head of a falcon; and Sekhmet, the lion-headed goddess of war and healing. By the time of the New Kingdom, some of these gods had changed a bit. For example, Amun and Ra were combined to become Amun-Ra, the main god of the ancient Egyptians.

MUMMIFICATION

When people think of ancient Egypt, they often think of mummies. Egypt was the perfect place for mummification—the process of making a mummy. The climate was hot and dry, so dead bodies dried out instead of **decaying** the way they did in most other parts of the world. By about 2600 BCE, the Egyptians were mummifying people on purpose to preserve their bodies because they thought the dead person would need their body in the next life.

Mummification was a long and expensive process. Only the very wealthy could afford to be mummified. It took 70 days and could only be done by specially trained priests. They knew the right prayers and **rituals**, and they

A mummy was made by carefully wrapping layers of linen cloth around the body.

also knew about the human body. This was important because part of mummification involved taking out organs that would decay quickly, such as the liver, lungs, and brain. The brain was taken out through the nose, so the priest had to be very skilled to get all of it out without ruining the person's face. The brain was thrown out, but the rest of the organs were preserved in special jars called canopic jars. The Egyptians believed the dead person would need these organs in the afterlife.

LIFE, NOT DEATH

Because of the great care the Egyptians took with their dead, some people think the ancient Egyptians were very focused on death. However, the truth is that they celebrated life. They believed that life continued after death. They turned the person into a mummy to preserve their body, and they filled the pyramids with food, drinks, jewelry, and other things to make the person comfortable and happy in the next life.

IMPORTANT ADVANCEMENTS

The Egyptians made many advancements in science and art, such as working with glass and metal. They made one of the world's first calendars. The ancient Egyptian calendar was based on the sun cycle. They were also believed to be the first people to create a kind of paper. It was made from a plant called papyrus, which is where the name "paper" comes from. However, it was very bumpy and fell apart with repeated use. The ancient Chinese invented modern papermaking.

The ancient Egyptians cared a lot about health, and they made some of the biggest medical advancements in history.

Egyptian furniture was some of the finest in the ancient world. These examples are in the Egyptian Museum in Cairo.

They invented toothbrushes and toothpaste, and they were thought to be the first to identify diabetes—a condition in which the body cannot use glucose, or sugar, properly. Egyptian doctors figured out that the urine of people with diabetes tasted sweet.

The ancient Egyptians also cared a lot about looking and smelling good, so they invented hairbrushes, wigs, and shaving. Because the ancient Egyptians liked to have fun, they also invented bowling!

No one knows who the Sea Peoples really were or where they came from, but experts know they attacked Egypt. This picture shows King Ramesses III beating the Sea Peoples in battle.

CHAPTER FOUR
THE FALL OF EGYPT

The New Kingdom was the last long period of peace and stability for ancient Egypt. After spending all its money on building projects and the military, Egypt was once again weakened. A group called the Sea Peoples attacked more than once while the civilization was weak. They never took control of Egypt, but these battles stopped ancient Egypt from returning to its full strength.

THIRD INTERMEDIATE AND LATE PERIODS

During the Third Intermediate Period, from 1069 to 664 BCE, the Egyptian government was often weak and had trouble keeping Egypt united. The Kush Empire from Nubia took over at one point, but it was later beaten by the Assyrian Empire. The Assyrians changed their mind about ruling Egypt and gave it back to the Egyptians. However, it was never as strong as it had once been, so instead of being known as the Fourth Kingdom, this time was called the Late Period.

In 525 BCE, the Persians attacked Egypt and took over. The Egyptians thought cats were sacred because they were living symbols of the goddess Bastet. The Persians knew this, so they painted cats on their shields and herded a large group of cats in front of their army toward the Egyptian army. The Egyptians did not want to hurt the cats, so the Persians won the battle. From then until the end of the Late Period, Egypt was under Persian rule.

THE PTOLEMAIC AND ROMAN PERIODS

In 332 BCE, Alexander the Great arrived in Egypt with his army. The Egyptians did not like being ruled by the Persians, so they let Alexander take the city without a fight. He left his mark on Egypt by creating a new city called Alexandria. Alexandria was home to the famous Library of Alexandria, a center of great learning. After Alexander's death, Alexandria became the new capital of Egypt and an important place for trade. This period of ancient Egypt was called the Ptolemaic Period after Alexander's general, a man named Ptolemy. Ptolemy started the Ptolemaic dynasty in Egypt after Alexander's death, and his family ruled for many years.

A GREEK QUEEN OF EGYPT

Cleopatra is one of the first names people think of when they think of ancient Egypt, so it makes sense that most people believe she was Egyptian. However, she was actually Greek! She was related to Ptolemy, who came from Greece with Alexander the Great. Even though she was not Egyptian, she loved Egypt, and she ruled there for almost 30 years. She was the first Ptolemaic ruler to learn the Egyptian language.

When Alexander the Great (*shown here*) took over Egypt, he made it part of one of the world's largest empires.

This carving shows Cleopatra (*left*) and her son (*right*).

Cleopatra was the last of the Ptolemaic dynasty and the last pharaoh of Egypt before it fell to the Roman Empire. Egypt's small army was too weak to fight off the Roman army. Egypt was part of the Roman Empire from 30 BCE until about 395 CE, when the Roman Empire was divided. This part of ancient Egyptian history is called the Roman Period.

The ancient Egyptian civilization lasted for almost 3,000 years. When the Roman Empire split in two in the late 4th century, Christianity became the official religion in Egypt, and many of the other ancient Egyptian ways of life were also lost. This is why, even though Egypt is still a country today, it is not the same as ancient Egypt.

HISTORY HAPPENED HERE

THE GREAT SPHINX OF GIZA

- A sphinx was a mythical creature with the head of a woman and the body of a lion. This statue has the face of the ruler who ordered it built.
- The Great Sphinx is one of the world's largest statues.
- Archaeologists think the statue used to be painted.

LUXOR TEMPLE

- This temple was built during the New Kingdom period.
- It sits where Thebes used to be. Today, the city is called Luxor.
- The temple was built to honor Amun, the king of the gods; his partner, Mut; and their son, Khons.

THE PYRAMIDS OF GIZA

- The biggest pyramid, called the Great Pyramid, was the tallest building in the world for 3,800 years.
- Each block in the Great Pyramid weighs about the same as a car.
- All of the pyramids, including the Great Pyramid, face north.

EVENTS DURING ANCIENT EGYPT

CA 5000 BCE	Small farms and villages form along the Nile River.
CA 3100 BCE	Upper Egypt and Lower Egypt are united into a single kingdom.
CA 2686–2181 BCE	The Old Kingdom
CA 2181–2125 BCE	First Intermediate Period
CA 2125–1650 BCE	The Middle Kingdom
CA 1650–1550 BCE	Second Intermediate Period
CA 1550–1069 BCE	The New Kingdom
CA 1069–664 BCE	Third Intermediate Period
CA 664–332 BCE	Late Period
332–30 BCE	Ptolemaic Period
30 BCE–395 CE	Roman Period

GLOSSARY

archaeologist: Someone who studies the tools and other objects left behind by ancient people.

culture: The beliefs and ways of life of a group of people.

decay: To break down or rot.

develop: To cause something to become bigger or more advanced.

expert: Someone who has a special skill or knowledge.

irrigation: The watering of a dry area by man-made means in order to grow plants.

palette: A thin board or rock.

ritual: A formal ceremony or series of acts that is always performed in the same way.

river delta: A low-lying plain near the mouth of a river that often has rich soil.

site: The place where something (such as a building) is, was, or will be located.

symbol: A picture, shape, or object that stands for something else.

tomb: A building above or below ground where a person's body is kept after they die.

unite: To cause two or more things to join together and become one thing.

FIND OUT MORE

BOOKS

Croy, Anita. *Ancient Egypt*. London, UK: Franklin Watts, 2021.

Green, Jen. *Ancient Egypt*. New York, NY: DK Publishing, 2020.

Loh-Hagan, Virginia. *Ancient Egypt*. Ann Arbor, MI: Cherry Lake Publishing Group, 2021.

WEBSITES

Ducksters: Ancient Egypt for Kids
www.ducksters.com/history/ancient_egypt.php
This website contains articles covering many topics about ancient Egypt, including its inventions, important people, and culture.

YouTube: Ancient Egypt for Kids
www.youtube.com/watch?v=lBYmOuajdC8
This video gives information about ancient Egypt along with photos of what the ruins of this civilization look like today.

Publisher's note to educators and parents: Our editors have carefully reviewed these websites to ensure that they are suitable for students. Many websites change frequently, however, and we cannot guarantee that a site's future contents will continue to meet our high standards of quality and educational value. Be advised that students should be closely supervised whenever they access the internet.

INDEX

A
Ahmose I, 15
Alexander the Great, 24
Amenemhat I, 13
Amun, 17
Amun-Ra, 18
Assyrian Empire, 23

C
Cleopatra, 24, 27

E
Early Dynastic Period, 7, 11

F
First Intermediate Period, 11

H
Hatshepsut, 15
Heka, 17
Hyksos, 13, 15

I
inventions/advancements, 20–21
Iry-Hor, 9

K
Kush Empire, 13, 23

L
Late Period, 23, 24
Lower Egypt, 5, 7, 9, 11, 13

M
Manetho, 7
Memphis, 7–9
Mentuhotep II, 13
Middle Kingdom, 11, 13
mummification, 18–20

N
Narmer, 9
New Kingdom, 15, 17, 23
Nile River, 5
Nubia, 13, 15, 23

O
Old Kingdom, 11
Osiris, 17

P
Persians, 23–24
Ptolemaic dynasty, 24, 27
Ptolemy, 24
Punt, 15
pyramids, 11, 13

R
Ra, 17
religion, 17–18, 27
Roman Empire, 27

S
Sea Peoples, 23
Second Intermediate Period, 15
Sekhmet, 17

T
Thebes, 13, 15
Third Intermediate Period, 23
Thutmose I, 15

U
Upper Egypt, 5, 11, 13

W
writing systems, 9

UNEARTHING ANCIENT CIVILIZATIONS

ANCIENT EGYPT REVEALED

BY DONNA REYNOLDS

Cavendish Square
New York

Published in 2023 by Cavendish Square Publishing, LLC
29 E. 21st Street, New York, NY 10010

First Edition

Library of Congress Cataloging-in-Publication Data

Names: Reynolds, Donna, author. | Reynolds, Donna. Unearthing ancient civilizations.
Title: Ancient Egypt revealed / by Donna Reynolds.
Description: New York : Cavendish Square Publishing, 2023. | Series: Unearthing ancient civilizations | Includes index.
Identifiers: LCCN 2021052047 | ISBN 9781502665980 (library binding) | ISBN 9781502665973 (paperback) | ISBN 9781502665126 (set) | ISBN 9781502665997 (ebook)
Subjects: LCSH: Egypt–History–To 332 B.C.–Juvenile literature. | Egypt–History–332-30 B.C.–Juvenile literature. | Egypt–Civilization–To 332 B.C.–Juvenile literature.
Classification: LCC DT83 .R455 2023 | DDC 932/.01–dc23/eng/20211029
LC record available at https://lccn.loc.gov/2021052047

Editor: Jennifer Lombardo
Copyeditor: Abby Young
Designer: Deanna Paternostro

The photographs in this book are used by permission and through the courtesy of: Cover, back cover Merydolla/Shutterstock.com; p. 4 bumihills/Shutterstock.com; pp. 6–7 Alvaro Lovazzano/Shutterstock.com; p. 8 Cholpan/Shutterstock.com; p. 10 Bist/Shutterstock.com; p. 12 Filippo Vanzo/Shutterstock.com; p. 14 Piotr Velixar/Shutterstock.com; p. 16 Charbonnier Thierry/Shutterstock.com; pp. 18–19 Andrea Izzotti/Shutterstock.com; p. 21 Orhan Cam/Shutterstock.com; p. 22 Universal History Archive/UIG/Bridgeman Images; p. 25 Nenad Nedomacki/Shutterstock.com; p. 26 Everett Collection/Shutterstock.com; p. 28 (top left) OAnderson/Shutterstock.com; p. 28 (top right) Prin Adulyatham/Shutterstock.com; p. 28 (bottom) sculpies/Shutterstock.com.

CPSIA compliance information: Batch #CSCSQ23: For further information, contact Cavendish Square Publishing LLC, New York, New York, at 1-877-980-4450.

Printed in the United States of America